60-WISE!

Your essential guide to enjoying an
independent life in later years

D1339774

Independent*Age*

Supporting older people at home

The charity that helps older people stay independent

The Royal United Kingdom Beneficent Association

Founded in 1863

Registered charity no. 210729

Royal Patron: HRH Princess Alexandra

ISBN 0-9541400-2-8

Copy by Sally Cox

Additional research by Jill Eckersley

Design by Neil Straker Creative

Printed in Great Britain

Published by

IndependentAge

Supporting older people at home

IndependentAge is a national charity which helps older people on low incomes to stay in their own homes, whether owned or rented. We provide a small regular income guaranteed for life and extra grants for emergencies and essentials. Local volunteers provide friendship and support.
Find out more about us by: visiting our website
www.independentage.org.uk; or writing to Jonathan Powell,
Chief Executive, **IndependentAge**, 6 Avonmore Road, London W14 8RL.

If you have found this guide useful, we would love to hear from you. Do you have any extra tips or information which would benefit fellow readers and which you would like to see included? Please let us know.

Please send your comments to:
60-Wise
IndependentAge, 6 Avonmore Road
London W14 8RL.

You don't have to give up your independence just because you're entering later life. That's the message of this guide commissioned by older people's charity, **IndependentAge**.

Even if you're finding it hard to make ends meet on your pension, the good news is there is a wealth of help available: specialised charities; numerous benefits, grants and discounts aimed specifically at the over-sixties which are often left unclaimed; and a whole range of sophisticated equipment to help you stay mobile and enjoying life.

The key is knowing what help exists and where to look – finding your way around the system.

That is where this down-to-earth guide comes in.

We trust that with the right information at your fingertips, you will be able to remain independent in your own home for many years to come.

If you do ever need to move - *the majority of people never need to move into a residential or nursing home* - we have included information on sheltered accommodation and how to find and pay for residential care.

Contents

Money Money Money

Struggling to make ends meet on your pension? Financial help is available if you know where to look.

Are you claiming all you can?

Even if you've never claimed benefits before, you may now be eligible.

If you or your partner are aged 60 or over, you could get extra money every week on top of your pension through the Government's **Pension Credit** scheme. Call freephone **0800 99 1234** to apply or visit **www.pensions.gov.uk/pensioncredit** for more information.

If your income is too high for you to receive Pension Credit, you may still be able to get help with your council tax through **Council Tax Benefit** and your rent through **Housing Benefit**. Ask for leaflet GL16 (rent) or GL17 (council tax) at your local social security office.

If you or a relative need help with dressing, washing, eating or moving around at home, you may be able to claim **Attendance Allowance** - paid to people over 65 **regardless of savings and income**. You must have needed help for six months to qualify. See social security leaflet DS 702 or call freephone **0800 88 22 00** for more information.

If you are under 65, you may qualify for **Disability Living Allowance**. Call the Benefits Enquiry Line on freephone **0800 220 674**.

How to find out more

- Ring the Benefits Enquiry Line on freephone **0800 220 674**

- Read *Pensioners' Guide - Making the most of government help and advice*. Tel **0845 6 065 065** for a copy or visit **www.pensions.gov.uk/pensioncredit**

- Read Help the Aged's free leaflet *Can you claim it?* Call **020 7278 1114** and ask for the information resources team

- Call the Age Concern Advice Line on freephone **0800 00 99 66** **www.ageconcern.org.uk**

- Ask at your local social security (Department for Work and Pensions) office, pension centre or Citizens Advice Bureau (CAB)

Need a helping hand to fill out the forms?

Some benefits forms, e.g. for Attendance Allowance, are long and appear daunting. Ask for specialist help if you need it from your local CAB or by calling **0800 88 22 00**.

Help to pay fuel bills

If you receive a gas or electricity bill you can't pay, don't panic. All regional electricity companies and British Gas have a policy of not disconnecting pensioners between 1st October and 31st March (the colder months). Tell your gas or electricity supplier at once, letting them know you're a pensioner.

Available in some parts of Britain, the **Staywarm** scheme for pensioners could save you money. For a fixed charge you use as much gas or electricity as you need. Payment is monthly or weekly by direct debit or at your local post office. **Freephone 0800 1 694 694** for a quotation. **www.staywarm.co.uk**

If you are on disability or income-related benefits, you can claim **Cold Weather Payments** - paid automatically when the temperature falls below 0°C for seven consecutive days.

Finally, everyone aged 60 or over and regardless of income can claim a **Winter Fuel Payment**. The money is paid automatically before Christmas with your state pension or benefit. Phone the Winter Fuel Payments Helpline for details on **0845 9 151515** or pick up form WFP1 from your local social security office.

Help to make your home warmer

Are you aged 60 or over and getting a disability or income-related benefit? You may be able to claim a Warm Front Team grant of up to £2,500 (England) or a Home Energy Efficiency Scheme (HEES) grant of up to £2,700 (Wales) to pay for insulation and heating improvements to your home. Call **0800 952 0600** (England) or **0800 316 2815** (Wales) or visit **www.eaga.co.uk**

Extra money to make ends meet

Did you know..?

- National Health Service (NHS) prescription charges and sight tests are free to people aged 60 or over

- if you live alone, you can claim a 25% Council Tax discount

- most local authorities offer free or reduced bus fares to older people. Contact your local council or Passenger Transport Executive. You'll find their number under Local Government in the phone book

- a Senior Railcard will give people of 60 or over reduced train fares

- National Express give discount fares to people aged 60 or over through their routesixty scheme – Telephone **08705 808080** for further details

- if you are 75 or over, you qualify for a free TV licence. The TV licensing information helpline is **0845 602 33 34**

Help to pay for glasses and teeth

People on pension credit can claim some financial help to pay for glasses and dental treatment. There are two types of pension credit: Guarantee Credit and Savings Credit. If you receive Guarantee Credit, you can claim free National Health Service dental treatment, wigs and fabric supports. You can also get vouchers towards the cost of glasses or contact lenses and refunds of necessary travel costs to hospitals for NHS treatment (including check-ups).

If you receive Savings Credit only, dental treatment may not be free but you will be able to claim some help with the items listed above. For more details, call **0800 555 777** or ask for leaflets HC11 and HC12 at a main post office or social security office.

Help from a charity

There may be a charity helping people from your profession, background or local area. For example, if you or your spouse worked in the meat industry, you may be able to apply for help from the Butchers' and Drovers' Charitable Institution on **020 7606 4106**.

The help provided by charities varies widely. Some such as **IndependentAge** on **020 7605 4200** provide regular income and grants to those who qualify; others may only offer free advice.

How to find out if there is a charity which could help you

- ask at your local library or CAB to see a copy of *Charities Digest* (Family Welfare Association)

- telephone Charity Search on **0117 982 4060**

- visit **www.charity-commission.gov.uk/registeredcharities**

If you live in Northern Ireland

- you'll find charities listed by area in the Bryson House Social Directory, 28 Bedford Street, Belfast, BT2 7FE. Call **028 9032 5835**

- or telephone the Northern Ireland Council for Voluntary Action on **028 9087 7777**

Raising income or capital from your home

If your home has appreciated since you bought it, it represents capital (money) tied up. You may have seen adverts in the papers for equity release schemes. There are two main types: with a **home reversion scheme**, you sell your home or part of it to a private company in exchange for a cash lump sum or monthly annuity income. With a **home income plan**, you take out a mortgage loan against your home and the money is used to buy an annuity which pays you a regular income for life.

Seek independent legal and financial advice first

Before even considering such a plan, think about all the issues e.g. what will happen if you later want to sell your home to move somewhere smaller? Age Concern's free factsheet no. 12 *Raising income or capital from your home* is helpful. Call freephone **0800 00 99 66** for a copy. Finally, find out if there's a charity which might be able to help - see pages 13 and 14. **IndependentAge**, for example, may be able to assist you with income even if you are a home-owner.

What to do if you can't pay your rent

If you cannot pay your rent, you may qualify for Housing Benefit (see page 9). Your local Department for Work and Pensions (DWP) can also help to pay service charges if you live in a flat but this assistance is means-tested. If you are already in rent arrears, you may need the help of an experienced debt counsellor to negotiate a settlement for you - see page 16.

Problems paying the mortgage

One solution might be to renegotiate the terms of your mortgage through an Independent Financial Adviser (IFA). You can find a local IFA through IFA Promotions Ltd. on freephone **0800 085 3250**. The DWP may be able to pay your mortgage interest and some service charges for you if you are a leaseholder receiving Pension Credit. See also **Help from a charity** (page 13) and **Help with debts** (page 16).

Help with debts

Debt can cause sleepless nights and the sooner you seek advice, the better. Many Citizens Advice Bureaux offer a free legal and debt counselling service. They can help to organise repayment and sometimes negotiate with creditors on your behalf to write off debt and cancel interest.

Where to find help and advice

National Debt Line (a registered charity)	gives free, self-help advice over the phone; publishes free factsheets including what to do if you have mortgage or rent arrears **www.nationaldebtline.co.uk**	**0808 808 4000** (9am to 9pm)
Consumer Credit Counselling Service (a registered charity)	provides free, independent counselling to help you solve debt problems, avoid bankruptcy and learn to handle money **www.cccs.co.uk**	**freephone 0800 138 1111**
The Community Legal Service	can tell you where to find good quality legal advice in your area **www.clsdirect.org.uk**	**0845 608 1122**

If you receive many catalogues in your mail, you may be tempted into more debt. To remove your name from mailing lists, write to the Mailing Preference Service, Freepost 29, LON 20771, London WIE 0ZT. **www.mpsonline.org.uk**

Never be tempted to take out a loan to pay off debts. This may prove very costly in the long run.

Finding help at home

As you get older, you may have difficulty in carrying out simple tasks you need to do on your own, such as taking a bath, climbing the stairs or preparing food. You may just need help for a while, for example, after you've had a fall or an operation. Or your problems may be longer-term. The questions to ask yourself are

- Do I need to move into more suitable accommodation such as a ground floor property? See section 7 *Thinking about moving?*
- Could my home be adapted to suit my needs? Would I manage where I am if I moved downstairs, had extra help or specialised equipment?

What you should do

If you've just come out of hospital, the hospital social worker should have made arrangements for your continuing care.

The British Red Cross (**www.redcross.org.uk**) can also help. You'll find the number of your nearest branch in your phone book.

Arrange to see your GP or practice nurse. Some practices have nurses who specialise in the care of older people.

What they can do

Your GP may be able to visit you at home if you find it hard to get to the surgery. The doctor can also refer you to other sources of professional help, for example

- an occupational therapist, who can assess your needs and work out how your home could be adapted to accommodate them
- a district or community nurse who can help with changing dressings, injections, general nursing care
- an incontinence adviser
- dentists, opticians, physiotherapy and chiropody services - though you will probably have to wait for these

Some aids, like wheelchairs, zimmer frames and bedpans are also available through the NHS. Again, you may have to wait, or go to an alternative source of help like your local branch of the British Red Cross.

Contact the **Social Services**. Their number is in the phone book, usually listed under the name of your local council. Ask to speak to the duty officer or to someone who specialises in the care of older people.

Provision varies around the country, and it helps to have plenty of patience and determination, as well as friends, relatives and/or your GP on your side! Having said that, Social Services departments can be very helpful.

They may be able to offer

■ an assessment of your needs (but you may have to wait for this)

■ home helps to help with housework and carers to assist with personal care such as bathing and hair-washing

■ Meals on Wheels if you find cooking difficult

■ laundry services

■ occupational therapy

■ information about day centres, where you can meet people and have a hot meal

There may be a waiting list for some or all of the services provided, and you may be asked for a contribution towards costs. It depends where you live. If you are not offered these services, don't be afraid to ask.

If you need
special equipment...

The good news is there is lots of it. Specialist companies now produce a huge variety of aids to make life more manageable for those with physical problems. These range from bespoke wheelchairs designed to prevent pressure sores developing, right down to long-handled combs and gadgets which help you pull your socks or stockings on.

You may have problems with **mobility**, either indoors or out. The NHS usually provides only basic wheelchairs. If you want a powered wheelchair, or a scooter, you will probably have to buy one. They can be bought second-hand from reputable suppliers, or even borrowed (see page 22 for details).

Stair lifts and powered bath seats can transform your life and increase your independence. Sometimes local authority grants are available to help you buy them. Your local branch of the British Red Cross may be able to lend you items such as wheelchairs on a short-term basis.

Both commercial companies and charities working with disabled people can give you information about all the other aids available. *See pages 22-26 for contact numbers.*

> **Don't be afraid to approach friends and neighbours.**
> **Most will be glad to lend a hand.**

The human touch

Apart from the help you get from the NHS and Social Services, there are plenty of volunteer organisations ready and willing to offer a little extra help and support to older people. Age Concern, Arthritis Care, Contact the Elderly, the Women's Royal Voluntary Service (WRVS), your local Council for Voluntary Service, local churches, synagogues and mosques may be able to help you.

A little extra

Many older people like to 'top-up' the free help (known as statutory provision) you get from Social Services with some private care. You could pay for this using money from your Attendance Allowance or other benefit. Or you may qualify for a grant from a charity. *See section 1, Money Money Money.*

Need more information?

Finding help
at home

Age Concern England	publish books and leaflets, run day centres and home visiting schemes **www.ageconcern.org.uk**	**0800 00 99 66**
Age Concern Scotland	advise on services in Scotland. Publish factsheets on a wide variety of topics	**0131 220 3345**
Arthritis Care	can give details of local help including home visiting schemes **www.arthritiscare.org.uk**	**020 7380 6500**
British Red Cross	(This is the British Red Cross, not the Red Cross which is different) can lend wheelchairs, commodes and walking frames. It operates transport and escort services for essential appointments and offers help to those just out of hospital as well as respite care in your own home **www.redcross.org.uk**	**020 7235 5454**
Chiltern Invadex	has a catalogue of showers, hoists, walk-in baths, grab rails, etc **www.chilterninvadex.co.uk**	**01869 365500**

Contact the Elderly	organise small Sunday get-togethers in private homes for frail elderly people with few social contacts. Free **www.contact-the-elderly.org.uk**	**Freephone 0800 716 543 01505 874 412** (Scotland)
The Continence Foundation 307 Hatton Square 16 Baldwins Gardens London EC1N 7RJ	Give expert advice on the phone and can refer you to local help. Or write confidentially to the Helpline Nurse, enclosing a SAE. **www.continence-foundation.org.uk**	Continence helpline **0845 345 0165**
DIAL UK	is a network of disability advice services , can refer you to local help **www.dialuk.info**	**01302 310123**
Disabled Living Centres Council	can refer you to local centres where you can try out equipment and products **www.dlcc.org.uk**	**0161 834 1044**
Disabled Living Foundation	offer factsheets on choosing equipment like stair lifts **www.dlf.org.uk**	**0845 130 9177**

The following organisations can offer help and advice

Foundations	has information on local Home Improvement Agencies which exist to help older people stay in their own homes. They can assess your needs and report on your eligibility for improvement grants **www.cel.co.uk/foundations**	**01457 891909**
Help the Aged	have leaflets and information sheets on everything from health problems to fire hazards, which are available from GP surgeries, community centres and Help the Aged shops nationwide. You can also try their Seniorline on freephone **0808 800 6565** or **0808 808 7575** (Northern Ireland) **www.helptheaged.org.uk**	**020 7278 1114** ask for the Information Resources Team
Homeshare (Registered charity, London only)	enables older people to stay in their own homes by sharing with a younger person. The tenant-carer performs light household duties in exchange for reduced rent. **www.homesharelondon.com**	**020 7376 4558**

The following organisations can offer help and advice

Keep Able	is a commercial company selling a vast range of equipment from wheelchairs to specially-designed cutlery by mail order. They also have nine stores in the Midlands and South of England **www.keepable.co.uk**	**08705 202122**
Remap	is a charity which designs customised aids. Helpful if you need specialised equipment you cannot buy elsewhere **www.remap.org.uk**	**0845 1300 456**
Ricability	produce independent consumer guides on easier living equipment. Braille, tape and large print versions available **www.ricability.org.uk**	**020 7427 2460**
Royal National Institute for the Blind	helpline offers practical support, advice and information on anything from talking books to household aids and can also refer you to local help **www.rnib.org.uk**	**0845 766 9999**

Need more information?

The following organisations can offer help and advice

Finding help at home

Organisation	Description	Contact
Royal National Institute for the Deaf	has booklets, including *Age Related Hearing Loss* and catalogues of equipment like textphones **www.rnid.org.uk**	helpline **0808 808 0123** (voiceline) or **0808 808 9000** (textline)
Shopmobility	can give details of the 250 nationwide schemes which allow you to hire or borrow manual or powered wheelchairs and scooters on a short or longer-term basis. **www.shopmobility.org.uk**	**08456 442446**
Stroke Association	provides information on stroke illness including recovery and rehabilitation **www.stroke.org.uk**	**0845 303 3100**
UK Home Care Association	will send a list of approved, local providers of care in your own home, from help with shopping to 24-hour nursing. A useful free leaflet *Choosing Care in your Home* is available from them **www.ukhca.co.uk**	**0208 288 1551**
Ways and Means	has a catalogue including kitchen, bathing and toileting aids **www.nrs-uk.co.uk**	**0845 606 0911**
Women's Royal Voluntary Service	run Meals on Wheels through local authorities and privately, social transport schemes, Books on Wheels and a Good Neighbour scheme for minor household repairs **www.wrvs.org.uk**	**01235 442900** (local numbers in phone book)

Keeping your affairs shipshape

While you are fit, you will want to go on managing your own affairs - collecting your pension, paying the bills - for as long as possible. But if circumstances should change, you will feel more comfortable if you appoint a trusted friend or relative to do this for you.

Help to collect social security benefits

If you are not well or mobile enough to go to the post office to collect your money, you can appoint a trusted person as your agent. Ask for leaflet GL21 *A helping hand for benefits?* at your local social security (DWP) office. **www.dss.gov.uk**

Help to operate your bank account

If you want to give somebody the power to operate your bank account, write a letter to your bank. Or ask your bank for a 'third party mandate' form.

If you are in hospital for a while or absent abroad

You can grant another person or persons Power of Attorney, which allows them to take care of your finances temporarily. See your solicitor.

If you become mentally incapacitated

An Enduring Power of Attorney allows someone else to take over your financial affairs if you become too mentally incapacitated to deal with them yourself. If you are the partner or carer of someone diagnosed with dementia, they should grant you Enduring Power of Attorney while they can still satisfy a solicitor that they can understand what they are signing. It doesn't have to come into force until they become mentally incapacitated, when it has to be registered with the Public Guardianship Office. See your solicitor or seek advice from the Alzheimer's Society on **0845 3000 336**.

Making a Will

You will want to make sure that your partner, family, friends and favourite charities are helped after your death. The only way to make sure this happens is to make a valid Will.

If you do not make a Will, your 'estate' - everything you own when you die - will be divided up according to a set formula. Your money and possessions may not be distributed as you would wish.

> **You cannot assume your spouse will inherit everything, even if you are married. If your estate is worth more than a certain amount, other relatives could have a call on it.**

It is particularly important to make a Will if your circumstances are at all complicated e.g.

- ■ you have no surviving blood relatives - in which case the Crown gets everything
- ■ you are not married to your partner
- ■ there are former spouses and/or stepchildren to consider

How to make a Will

Find a reliable solicitor. Ask friends or family or consult your local Citizens' Advice Bureau. Call three local firms and ask for a quotation. Solicitors' charges vary from £100-£150 for a simple Will to £1,000 for a complex Will involving a large estate.

Before you see the solicitor, work out how much you are worth. It could surprise you! Take into account all

- property
- possessions
- life assurance policies
- savings accounts
- investments
- family heirlooms
- jewellery

Take away any debts such as a mortgage or credit cards and what is left is your estate. You will want to provide for dependants or perhaps leave money in trust for grandchildren under 18. You can leave someone

- a **specific legacy** - an item such as a painting or item of jewellery

- or a **pecuniary legacy**, which means a sum of money

Other instructions

- a gift to a charity. To avoid confusion, always give the charity registration number

- any wishes about donating an organ

- the kind of funeral you would prefer (put this in your Will or in a separate letter which you keep with it)

- money to pay for your pet's upkeep. (You cannot leave money to pets but you can specify a person to look after them)

Appointing executors

Executors are the people who make sure your wishes are carried out. Solicitors and banks will do this for you but will charge so you may prefer to appoint friends or relatives. It is legal for your executors to benefit from your Will.

Your solicitor will answer any questions you have and also help draft your Will so that your intentions are unambiguous. Otherwise, a bequest may 'fail', for instance if you have willed your 'favourite gold bracelet' to your 'favourite niece' without being more specific. The money and other assets left over once all debts, legacies and expenses have been paid is called the residue and may be left to one person, divided among relatives and friends or left to charity, as you wish.

Legally your Will must be **witnessed** by two people who must both be present when you sign it. Neither they nor their spouses may benefit from the Will.

Inheritance Tax is payable on estates worth more than a certain amount, currently £263,000. Bequests to spouses and charities are exempt. Avoiding Inheritance Tax is possible but does not benefit you personally, only your heirs. To find out how to do this, take legal advice.

Keeping your Will up to date

You should review your Will every few years, especially if your circumstances change. Never alter a Will except by consulting a solicitor and adding what is known as a Codicil. If there have been several major changes in your life you might need to consider making a new Will. Keep your Will in a safe place and make sure your family and/or executors know where to find it.

Living Wills, known as **Advance Directives**, are statements of your wishes about medical treatments to be given or withheld if you suffer from serious, incurable and/or terminal illness and are unable, at the time, to make decisions about your treatment. Signing a Directive lets your doctors and family know exactly what your wishes are in such circumstances. See your solicitor.

If you live in Scotland, the law relating to Wills and inheritance is different, as are some of the legal terms used. There are some differences in the law in Northern Ireland also. But making a Will is just as important wherever you live.

How to find out more

Help the Aged Seniorline	can send you a free Will Information Pack **www.helptheaged.org.uk**	**0808 800 6565**
Age Concern	has free factsheets on *Making your Will* (factsheet 7, 7s for Scotland) and *Legal arrangements for managing financial affairs* (factsheet 22, 22s for Scotland) **www.ageconcern.org.uk**	**0800 00 99 66**

How to find out more

Which? Books	have a range of useful publications including *What to do when someone dies* paperback, £10.99, and *Wills and probate* paperback, £11.99 Both the books, but not the Will pack, have sections on Scottish and Northern Irish law. **www.which.net**	Freephone **0800 252 100** or from good bookshops
The Natural Death Centre	can provide information about Living Wills and eco funerals e.g. woodland burials **www.naturaldeath.org.uk**	**0871 288 2098**
The Organ Donation Literature Line	can provide information about organ donation **www.uktransplant.org.uk**	**0845 6060 400**
The Alzheimer's Society	has information about Wills and arranging Powers of Attorney **www.alzheimers.org.uk**	Helpline **0845 3000 336**
Alzheimer's Scotland	has information about Wills and arranging Powers of Attorney in Scotland. Scottish law is different **www.alzscot.org.uk**	24-hour helpline **0808 808 3000**
Solicitors for the Elderly	a nationwide group who specialise in acting for older people **www.solicitorsfortheelderly.com**	**01992 471 568**

Safe and secure at home

Here's some good news. Despite what you may imagine, *there is less crime against older people than any other age group.* In fact, you are more likely to injure yourself in a fall at home than to get hurt in a burglary. But there are many steps you can take to feel safer and more secure.

Improving your home security

One of the best safeguards against crime is to know your neighbours and keep their phone numbers handy. If you don't know your neighbours, join your local Neighbourhood Watch scheme – for details, call the Crime Prevention Officer at your local police station. The Crime Prevention Officer will also be able to give you expert advice on making your home more secure.

Some local Age Concern groups will supply and fit spy-holes for front doors free and also fit (though not supply) door safety chains, window locks and smoke alarms for pensioners who ask for them.

Safe and secure at home

Real or bogus caller?

If the person who comes to read the meter is genuine, they will know your account number. So keep an old gas or electricity bill in a handy place by the front door and ask the caller to confirm your account number for you. Another good tip is to ask the gas, electricity or water company if they run a password scheme.

Always slip the safety chain on the front door before you open it to a stranger.

Crimes by door-to-door callers are slightly more common if you live in council or social housing. This may be because tenants feel more obliged to let callers in - particularly if they look official. If in doubt, keep them out!

Unsolicited phone calls

Unsolicited phone calls can be inconvenient and annoying. You may answer the phone and find no-one at the other end. This often happens when salespeople use the automatic systems to dial several numbers at the same time. They speak to the first person who answers and cut the rest off.

If you would rather not receive unsolicited sales calls, register with the **Telephone Preference Service on 0845 070 0707**

Community alarm systems

What will happen if you have a fall, stroke or heart attack at home and cannot phone for help?

Over a million people in Britain - not all in the best of health - remain independent thanks to a community alarm system. The terms *social alarm, care-line, care-phone* or *lifeline* are also used. They work like this: you press an alarm button on a wrist-band or pendant; this sends a signal from your home alarm unit to the call centre; your medical details appear on screen and the operator talks to you. Depending on your circumstances, the operator calls a trusted friend or relative who has a key and/or dials the emergency services.

Finding an alarm scheme in your area

First try your local authority (housing department) or housing association to see what they provide. If that fails, contact the Association of Social Alarm Providers for a local recommendation. Write to ASAP, 4 Beaufort House, Beaufort Court, Sir Thomas Longley Road, Rochester, Kent ME2 4FB, or call them on **0870 043 4052**, or e-mail them at admin@asap-uk.org.

If money is a problem, say so
The National Benevolent Fund for the Aged (**www.nbfa.org.uk**) lends alarms to pensioners on a low income. Tel **020 7828 0200**. Other charities which can help with an alarm and/or telephone include Friends of the Elderly, Help the Aged, Invalids at Home and The Royal British Legion (Earl Haig Fund in Scotland).

The greatest threat to your safety – you!

Every day over 600 people over 65 are hurt in a fall. If this leads to a fracture, it can threaten your independence permanently so

- keep as mobile and active as you can
- ask someone fitter than you to change light bulbs or go up in the loft
- get up slowly from your bed or armchair to avoid dizziness
- keep hallways and stairs well lit and clear of clutter
- wear close-fitting shoes, not loose slippers
- in your bathroom, get a non-slip mat and grip rail, have a fitted carpet, not lino, and leave the door unlocked

Avoiding Slips, Trips and Broken Hips (Department of Trade and Industry) gives you more information about how to avoid accidental falls at home.
This is available to download at **www.dti.gov.uk/publications**

Safe and secure at home

Free carbon monoxide safety checks

Faulty gas appliances can leak poisonous carbon monoxide which you can't detect until it's too late. A carbon monoxide detector costs about £5 at DIY stores and lasts about three months. Or ask your gas or electricity company if they offer free gas safety checks to pensioners. Many do.

Fire prevention

The commonest causes of house fires are cigarettes and chip pans so

■ never smoke in bed and take great care with cigarettes

■ don't use chip pans at home. Buy oven chips or use the chip shop

Two other steps you can take are

■ do not use electric blankets which are over 10 years old or show wear and tear. Some local authorities run free electric blanket testing days. Ask your local Trading Standards department

■ get a smoke alarm - look for British Standard number BS 5446 and batteries lasting 10 years. In some areas, the local Fire Brigade will install smoke alarms for pensioners free of charge. It could save your life

Home and not so alone

It is natural to be more anxious about security if you live alone and cannot share your troubles. If your life is not as full as it could be, consider a day centre or a class where you'll meet other people. Ask at your local library or adult education college or contact the University of the Third Age (**www.u3a.org.uk**) on **020 8466 6139**.

If you are lonely because you have recently been bereaved, CRUSE Bereavement Care on **0870 167 1677** may be able to recommend a local support group. **www.crusebereavementcare.org.uk**

The St. Vincent de Paul Society **020 7935 9126** (**www.svp.org.uk**) and Contact the Elderly **0800 716 543** (**www.contact-the-elderly.org.uk**) provide companionship and home visits to less mobile, older people.

Make new friends by becoming a volunteer yourself.

Contact Volunteering England on **0845 305 6979**
(**www.volunteering.org.uk**). Or look up your local volunteer bureau in the
phone book.

Last but not least, ever considered going back to work?

Minute-taking, market research, teaching, proofreading, consultancy
and working as a meeter-and-greeter for professional associations are
among the part-time openings available to older workers. The National
Trust (**0870 609 5380**) takes on seasonal paid workers (up to the age
of 70) at peak times. Part-time earnings by retired people count as
taxable income so the Inland Revenue booklet IR121 *Income Tax and
Pensioners* may be helpful. Call **0845 9000 404** for a free copy.

Where to find more information

Home security and crime prevention

Help the Aged have excellent free leaflets on *Security in Your Home,
Safety in Your Home, Living Alone Safely* and *Fire*. Call **020 7278 1114**
and ask for the information department. **www.helptheaged.org.uk**

Age Concern has a free factsheet (no. 33) entitled *Crime Prevention for
older people*. Call **0800 00 99 66**. **www.ageconcern.org.uk**

If you have been the victim of a crime, phone the Victim Support
helpline for sympathetic help and advice on **0845 30 30 900**.
www.victimsupport.org.uk

Voluntary work

Retired and Senior Volunteer Programme (RSVP) has a range of activities for older and retired people, for example, helping in schools, doctors' surgeries and museums.
Call **020 7643 1385** (England), **0131 622 7766** (Scotland), **02920 390477** (Wales) or visit **www.csv-rsvp.org.uk**. In Northern Ireland, call Voluntary Services, Belfast on **00 353 405 5776**.

REACH on **020 7582 6543** (**www.reach-online.org.uk**) finds part-time, expenses-only jobs anywhere in Britain for retired people with business or professional experience who want to work as volunteers for charities.

Learning opportunities

Learndirect has information about learning opportunities in your area. Call freephone **0800 100 900** (Britain, Wales, Northern Ireland) or visit **www.learndirect.co.uk**. In Scotland, call **0808 100 9000**.

Coping with confusion

Someone in your household may be suffering from **confusion or forgetfulness**. The symptoms are: loss of short term memory; repeating themselves; mood changes; problems carrying out everyday tasks; and disorientation. It can be lonely trying to cope but there is a lot of help available.

What you should do

Before jumping to conclusions, get a doctor's diagnosis - people over 75 are entitled to a home visit from their GP. If you cannot convince the confused person they need to see a doctor, make an appointment to discuss something else they may have, such as a cold. Call the GP first to explain the situation.

Coping with confusion

43

Reasons for forgetfulness

We all forget things sometimes and absent-mindedness doesn't necessarily mean you or the person you are concerned about have Alzheimer's disease or any other form of dementia. Other conditions causing confusion include

- depression, which can be treated

- thyroid problems, which can be treated

- dehydration, which can be treated by drinking plenty of fluids

- some medicines which affect people in this way

Depression is common in elderly people and the symptoms are very similar to those associated with dementia. Modern treatments have few side effects and can bring about a dramatic improvement.

What is Alzheimer's disease?

Alzheimer's is a progressive, degenerative brain disease, which gradually destroys brain cells. People with Alzheimer's slowly lose their ability to remember, communicate, recognise others and deal with everyday life. Although there is no cure, much can be done to improve the quality of life for people with dementia and their carers in the early stages of the disease.

Published by the Alzheimer's Society, **I'm told I have dementia** is a practical booklet full of helpful tips and contact numbers. Free to people who have been diagnosed with any kind of dementia. Call the Alzheimer's Society information department on **0845 3000 336** to order a copy. **www.alzheimers.org.uk**

Other kinds of dementia

Alzheimer's disease is the most common form of dementia but there are other kinds including

- **multi-infarct dementia**, which is caused by a series of small strokes
- **Pick's disease,** a rare form of dementia
- **Huntington's disease**, an inherited condition

People with HIV infection, Parkinson's disease, or severe alcohol problems may also develop dementia. Dementia currently affects about 700,000 people in the UK. About half of these (55%) have Alzheimer's.

Is there any treatment?

There is lots of research but no cure yet. Three drugs, Aricept, Exelon and Reminyl are licensed for use in the UK and appear to help some people with early Alzheimer's. Speak to your GP or call the Alzheimer's Society.

> The Alzheimer's Society has over 250 local support groups around the country. Phone their helpline on **0845 3000 336** for details of your nearest branch or visit **www.alzheimers.org.uk**

Living with Alzheimer's

In its early stages, the condition can be managed, and help is available from the NHS, Social Services and voluntary organisations. Both the person with dementia and their carer should get a care assessment from Social Services or their GP. Your GP can put you in touch with Social Services, the Community Mental Health team or the district nurse. Provision varies around the country but you may be entitled to

- ■ a home help

- ■ Meals on Wheels

- ■ some home nursing care

- ■ physiotherapy and occupational therapy if appropriate

- ■ chiropody services

- ■ continence advice and laundry services

- ■ special equipment such as commodes

You may have to contribute to the cost of some of these services.

Caring for a person with confusion

Those who look after confused elderly people every day are entitled to their own care assessment. This will probably include **respite care** of some kind. Again, provision varies but could include

- home care, where someone comes in for an hour or two to give the carer a break

- day centres, where patients can spend some time away from home, perhaps enjoying hobbies, visits or just a change of scenery

- holiday breaks, for patient, carer or both

Some of this help is provided by Social Services, or by voluntary organisations like the Alzheimer's Society or the Winged Fellowship Trust, who run special holidays for people with Alzheimer's (telephone numbers shown on page 51).

A familiar environment

People with Alzheimer's disease cope much better in a familiar environment. Their condition may get worse if they have to move.

Managing difficult behaviour

People with Alzheimer's can behave in ways that are difficult to manage, especially as the disease progresses. They may: forget they have eaten and raid the fridge; get up in the middle of the night and wander off; leave taps running or fires blazing; or forget how to handle money. Worse still, they may become aggressive if they think someone else is 'taking over', especially if they have no clear recollection of who you are. The Alzheimer's Society has a range of advice sheets covering common problems, from *Driving and Dementia* to *Aggressive Behaviour*. Carers' groups are another good source of advice and support.

Financial help

People with dementia are entitled to help from the State. Your social worker, or the local Citizens' Advice Bureau, should be able to advise you. Much depends on your circumstances but, as a general rule, those under 65 may claim **Disability Living Allowance** and those over 65 may claim **Attendance Allowance**. Ring the Benefits Enquiry Line on freephone **0800 220 674**.

If your spouse has been diagnosed with dementia and is receiving Attendance Allowance, you may claim a 25% Council Tax discount.

Managing the person's money

An Enduring Power of Attorney (EPA) allows a trusted person to take over your financial affairs if you become too mentally incapacitated to handle them yourself. You can make an EPA if you have a diagnosis of dementia but must be able to satisfy a solicitor you can understand what you are signing. Two Alzheimer's Society information sheets – which you can download from their website – are helpful: *Enduring power of attorney and receivership* and *Financial and legal tips*. Or call **0845 3000 336** for advice.

Telling people about the situation

It is wise to let neighbours, local shopkeepers, even the police know the situation, especially if the person with dementia is liable to wander off. Inform your gas, electricity, water and telephone company. If they know a customer has mental health problems, they won't cut off services without consulting carers.

Residential care

Dementia is a progressive condition and the time will probably come when even the most devoted carer needs to think about residential care for their loved one - either in a residential or nursing home. The main difference between these two types of accommodation is that nursing homes have to be able to provide 24-hour nursing care. Not all people with dementia need this.

You can obtain information about homes which care for patients with dementia from

■ your GP

■ Social Services

■ the Elderly Accommodation Counsel

■ the Alzheimer's Society

■ Counsel and Care

■ the Relatives' and Residents' Association

Visit several homes before making a decision. The Relatives' and Residents' Association can provide a useful checklist of things to look for.

Help for people with dementia and their carers

Alzheimer's Society	have over 250 local support groups nationwide. Publish useful literature. **www.alzheimers.org.uk**	**Helpline 0845 3000 336**
Alzheimer Scotland-Action on Dementia	can put you in touch with your nearest support group. Publish helpful leaflets **www.alzscot.org.uk**	**24-hour helpline 0808 808 3000**
Carers UK	provide information and support to carers of all kinds **www.carersonline.org.uk**	**020 7490 8818**
Princess Royal Trust for Carers	have 102 carers' centres all around the country **www.carers.org**	**020 7480 7788**
Crossroads Care Attendance Scheme	specialise in home carers **www.crossroads.org.uk**	**01788 573653** **0141 226 3793 (Scotland)**
Vitalise	can accommodate elderly, mentally frail people and their carers at their holiday centres **www.vitalise.org.uk**	**0845 345 1972**

Help with choosing residential care

Counsel and Care Advice Line www.counselandcare.org.uk	**0845 300 7585**
Elderly Accommodation Counsel www.housingcare.org	**020 7820 1343**
Relatives' and Residents' Association www.relres.org	**020 7359 8136**

Coping with confusion

Residential care providers

Abbeyfield www.abbeyfield.com	**01727 857536** **0131 225 7801** (Scotland)
Anchor Housing www.anchorhousing.org.uk	**08457 758595**
Hanover Housing Association www.hanover.org.uk	**01784 446000** **0131 557 0598** (Scotland)
MHA Care Group www.mha.org.uk	**01332 296200**

When someone dies

If you have never had to deal with a death before, it is helpful to have an idea of what must be done. Show this section to the friend or relative assisting you with the arrangements. There are also useful numbers below to support you through the challenging times ahead.

What to do first

If the cause of death is clear, the doctor who attended the person who died will give you a Medical Certificate. If the cause of death is unclear, for instance, if the death was sudden, the doctor will refer the death to a coroner.

The next step, registering the death

You need to register the death within five days at the Registrar of Births and Deaths for the sub-district in which it occurred. If the death was referred to the coroner, their authority is needed - known as the 'pink form.' The coroner usually sends this directly to the Registrar.

■ You need to produce the Medical Certificate and full details about the person who died including their place of birth, marriage, state pension, occupation and spouse's occupation

The registrar will give you

■ The Green Form (Certificate for Burial or Cremation) unless the coroner has given you an Order for Burial (form 101) or form E (Certificate for Cremation)

■ A Certificate of Registration of Death (BD8(rev)). This is for Social Security purposes only

The registrar will also give you the Death Certificate. You need this to obtain probate, pensions claims, insurance policies, savings certificates and premium bonds. Extra copies - which you have to pay for - can be useful. It's cheaper to ask for them now.

Do not arrange the funeral until

■ you have found out if there's a Will showing the person's wishes e.g. burial or cremation

■ you know who is paying

■ you are sure the death does not have to be reported to the coroner. Bodies may not be cremated until the cause of death is clear

■ you know which would be more acceptable - flowers or donations

Paying for the funeral

A funeral is paid out of the dead person's estate. It can be expensive. So look carefully through their papers to see if they had an

■ occupational pension scheme, trade union (or other professional body) membership that might pay a lump sum to help with funeral costs

■ life insurance policy which will provide a lump sum payment if someone dies before a certain age

■ a pre-paid funeral plan

If you or your partner receive benefits, you may be able to get a **Social Fund Funeral Payment**. This will have to be paid back from any estate of the person who died. Ask for form SF200 at your social security office.

Finding a funeral director

Look in your parish newsletter, Yellow Pages or ask for recommendations. Or phone the National Association of Funeral Directors (**0121 711 1343**), or the Society of Allied and Independent Funeral Directors (**01279 726 777**), all of whom can give you details of members in your area.

Don't be afraid to get two or three quotations, or to ask for a basic package, even if it is not offered. If you do not have the heart for this, ask a friend to help. Don't be persuaded to have a more elaborate or expensive funeral than you really want or can afford. Charges for burials and cremations vary around the country. Expect to pay from £1,100 for a basic package including a coffin, hearse and one limousine for the mourners.

You do not have to use a funeral director. For advice about alternative funerals and cremations, phone the Natural Death Centre on **0871 288 2098**. For example, some people like the idea of a woodland burial and there are now 180 woodland burial sites around the country.

When someone dies

Where to find more information

■ Read leaflet D49, *What to do after a death in England and Wales*. This free, step-by-step guide covers most circumstances from organ donation to death abroad and DIY funerals. It is available from local benefit offices, Citizens' Advice Bureaux, hospitals and doctors' surgeries.

■ In Scotland, leaflet D49S, *What to do after a death in Scotland*, gives the same information

■ *What to do when someone dies* (Which Books, £10.99) gives information and advice on arranging a funeral. Call freephone **0800 252 100** to order a copy.

■ The Help the Aged leaflet *Bereavement* obtainable from Information Dept, Help the Aged, 207-221 Pentonville Road, London N1 9UZ includes information on arranging a funeral. Tel: **020 7278 1114**

■ The Cremation Society has a free leaflet *What you should know about cremation* available from them at 2nd floor, Brecon House, 16-16A Albion Place, Maidstone, ME14 5DZ. Tel: **01622 688292**.

When someone dies

Dealing with the person's estate

The person who deals with the deceased's property and possessions is known as the personal representative. They are also called: the Executor (if named as such in the Will) or the Administrator (if there's no Will).

You need a legal document to confirm you are allowed to deal with the dead person's assets. This is called probate (for executors) or 'letters of administration' (for administrators). See a solicitor or get Form PA2 *How to obtain probate* from a CAB or probate registry (listed under P in the business numbers section of the phone book).

The personal representative pays the deceased's debts, taxes and expenses including funeral costs out of the estate and then shares out the rest of the estate.

You may not need a formal legal document or solicitor's help if the whole estate comes to less than £5,000.

How to find out more

Read Age Concern's free factsheet no. 14 *Dealing with someone's estate.* Tel **freephone 0800 00 99 66.**

Other important things to do

If you have lost a close relative, you should change your Will. See page 29.

If the person who died was receiving a state pension or any Department of Work and Pensions (DWP) benefit, tell your local social security office as soon as possible. Otherwise, if DWP have accidentally overpaid, they will later want the money back.

Remove the deceased person's name from mailing lists by writing to The Mailing Preference Service, Freepost 29, LON 20771, London W1E 0ZT. Tel **0845 703 4599** or, if the person lived alone, tell the Post Office.

Financial help for people who are left

The loss of a family member may leave you poorer. Even if you have never claimed benefits before, you may now be eligible - see page 9 of this booklet.

Where to find practical advice, support and comfort

CRUSE Bereavement Care	provides counselling, advice, information and social contact through more than 196 local branches to anyone bereaved **www.crusebereavementcare.org.uk**	**0870 167 1677**
The National Association of Widows	has over 40 branches. It can put you in touch with other widows in your area, and refer you to other forms of help **www.widows.uk.net**	**0247 663 4848**
The Samaritans	provide someone to talk to in confidence if you are suicidal and despairing **www.samaritans.org.uk**	**08457 90 90 90** (or look for a local number in your phone book)
The War Widows Association of Great Britain	offers advice, help and support to war widows, widowers and their dependants **www.warwidowsassociation.org.uk**	**0870 241 1305**

Thinking about moving?

One way of maintaining, or even increasing, your independence, is to move house, usually to a smaller, more manageable or more conveniently situated home. Retirement housing - for sale or rent - is an option for active and independent older people who don't need personal or nursing care, but who like the reassurance of knowing that help is at hand if it should ever be needed.

Retirement housing comes in many forms - cottages, flats and bungalows. Some developments are sold to over-55s only but offer no special facilities. Others, usually known as sheltered housing, have a resident manager who acts as a good neighbour, but can't normally give personal care (e.g. help with bathing and dressing) or nursing care.

Sheltered housing can be bought or rented. There is also a service charge which covers items like gardening, maintenance, repairs, and the upkeep of common areas. Sheltered homes are completely self-contained but there are often some shared facilities like residents' lounges, laundry rooms, and guest suites for visitors. For those who need a little more support, there are developments which do offer help with personal care, meals etc. These are sometimes known as **very sheltered housing**, **assisted living** or **extra care** schemes.

Making the decision

Thinking ahead can be useful. You may not always want the responsibility of a large garden, or to have to walk a mile to the post office.

Ask yourself

- Do I want to stay in the same area, near to my friends?

- Do I prefer city or country life?

- Do I want to be nearer to my family?

- What sort of property would suit me best? A bungalow? A cottage? A flat? Do I need a home which is adapted for a wheelchair?

- Do I need somewhere which accepts pets?

Buying or renting?

Retirement housing can be bought directly from developers, or second-hand through high street or specialist estate agents.

It can also be rented from local authorities and housing associations, sometimes known as Registered Social Landlords (RSLs).

To help those on low incomes, there are

- **shared ownership** schemes where you buy an interest in the property and pay rent on the rest
- **leasehold schemes** for the elderly where you buy 70% of the property and the housing association owns the rest
- **lifetime occupancy schemes** where you buy the right to live in the property for your lifetime

Councils and RSLs all try to let to those in most need, either because their present housing is unsuitable; they have health problems; are on lower incomes; or want to be nearer friends and family.

What you should do

Contact the developer, housing association, or estate agent and ask for an appointment to see the homes that interest you.

As well as checking room sizes, the layout of the flat and the general atmosphere, you will want to find out

- what expenses are covered by the service charges and how much you will have to pay, both now and in the future
- what special features are incorporated into the design, e.g. non-slip flooring, grab rails in the bathroom, possible wheelchair access, a lift if the property is not on the ground floor
- what arrangements could be made for extra care if you become frailer/less able to cope
- whether residents do a lot of socialising or prefer to keep themselves to themselves
- the arrangements for visitors - if there is a guest suite and how much it costs
- how near the development is to shops, doctor's surgery and transport
- the parking arrangements for your own car or visitors
- whether pets are welcome

Thinking about moving?

It's important, too, to meet the **resident manager**. Is this someone you can get along with? Would you be happy to turn to them in an emergency?

Some developments encourage would-be residents to stay for a couple of nights in the visitors' suite to see how they like the place.

If you need more help

Sheltered housing is most suitable for active elderly people, although you are entitled to exactly the same help from your GP and Social Services if you live in sheltered housing as you are living in your former home (see section 2 for details).

If you need more care, for instance, help with bathing and dressing or you have problems preparing meals for yourself, you might find that **very sheltered housing**, **assisted living**, or **extra care** might be more appropriate for you.

These are schemes where, although you live in your own flat or bedsitter with its own facilities, some meals are provided for you, as well as personal care.

Would you like more information?

The Elderly Accommodation Counsel on **020 7820 1343** is an independent charity which can help older people choose the most suitable home, including sheltered and extra-care housing.

Read **Age Concern's** free factsheet no 2 *Retirement housing for sale* Call freephone **0800 00 99 66**.

Help the Aged's Seniorline on **0808 800 65 65** is a free information service for older people. Help the Aged also produces a range of free advice leaflets including *Housing Matters* – on housing options.

Among the developers and housing associations providing sheltered housing are

Abbeyfield	offer very sheltered housing in private, self-furnished rooms with meals provided, but with no personal or nursing care except in an emergency. Fees are modest **www.abbeyfield.com**	**01727 857 536** **0131 225 7801** (Scotland)
Anchor Housing	is a leading, not-for-profit provider of housing, care and support services all over England with retirement housing for sale and rent, as well as residential and nursing care, and support services **www.anchorhousing.org.uk**	**08457 75 85 95**
Dewi Sant Housing Association	provide sheltered housing in Swansea, Pembrokeshire and Carmarthenshire **www.ctdewisant.org.uk**	**01639 887 417**
Hanover Housing	provide retirement flats and bungalows to rent all over Britain, and also extra care accommodation which can include both personal care and meals **www.hanover.org.uk**	**01784 446 000** **0131 557 0598** (Scotland)

Thinking about moving?

Among the developers and housing associations providing sheltered housing are

McCarthy & Stone	are the country's leading builders of retirement flats to buy, with more than 2,000 developments all over Britain. **www.mccarthyandstone.co.uk**	**01202 292480**
MHA Care Group	offer self-contained rented flats in England, Scotland and Wales, all of which have a Scheme Manager **www.methodisthomes.org.uk**	**01332 296200**
New Leaf	is a specialist social landlord with 2,500 retirement properties to rent, mostly in the North of England **www.placesforpeople.co.uk/newleaf**	**0845 604 44 46**
Retirement Homesearch	are specialist estate agents handling the sale/purchase of retirement property all over the UK **www.retirementhomesearch.co.uk**	**0870 600 55 60** **0141 248 2846** Scotland

Residential and nursing home care

Two out of three older people never need to go into an 'old people's home'. If you are considering residential care, first look at the alternatives

- Could you stay in your own home with helpers coming in and special equipment? See section 2, *Finding Help at Home*.

- Could you stay independent a little longer by moving to sheltered or very sheltered housing? See section 7, *Thinking about moving?*

If residential care really is the best option, try to be positive. Once you settle in, you may relish the extra security, comfort and company a home provides. There is lots of free advice and support available to help you find and pay for the right home.

Which kind of home?

There are three types of home

A **nursing home** must have a qualified nurse on duty 24 hours a day. This is the best choice if you are extremely frail, bedridden or need a lot of attention from a doctor or nurse.

A **residential home** cannot provide 24-hour nursing care but can provide 24-hour supervision. If required, staff help with washing, dressing and going to the toilet.

A **dual-registered home** has both nursing and residential care residents. This can be useful if you need more care later on.

What will it cost?

The national average cost for a residential home is £345 and for a nursing home £496 a week (Laing & Buisson survey 2004). Fees vary a great deal and are rising rapidly.

Expect to pay more

- in the Southeast and Southwest of England and other areas where property prices are high
- where there are fewer homes so less competition
- if luxury extras such as a hydrotherapy pool are offered

The terms and conditions of your contract should tell you exactly what the price includes.

What to do next

Contact the Social Services department (or the social work department in Scotland) of your local authority. Ask them to assess your care needs.

Do this even if you can afford to pay for a home privately.

In time you may use up your savings and need help from Social Services. They will be able to help more quickly and easily if you have an assessment now.

Finding a home

The Social Services department of your local council should be able to send you a list of residential homes. The Health Authority can provide a list of registered nursing homes.

You could also ask

- your GP
- family and friends
- your local Citizens' Advice Bureau
- your local Age Concern office
- the Community Health Council
- your local library
- your solicitor

> If you have problems finding a suitable home for a person with dementia, turn to page 50 or speak to the Elderly Accommodation Counsel on **020 7820 1343**.

Paying for care

The rules on paying for residential care are complicated. If after reading this section, you are still confused and would like someone to explain things, call one of the organisations listed on page 82.

Who pays what?

Once the local authority has agreed you need to go into residential care, you pay your contribution directly to the home or to the local authority. The amount you pay depends how much money they think you have after you have completed a *financial assessment*.

If you have more than £20,000 in savings, you have to pay full fees. Your home, if you own it, counts as savings unless one of the people shown on page 75 lives there.

The value of your home doesn't count for the first 12 weeks you are living full-time in a care home. Social services will help pay your fees for 12 weeks or until your house is sold, *whichever is sooner and provided your other savings are below £20,000.*

This is called the 12 week property disregard.

If, for example, you sell your house after four weeks, the disregard will cease. But social services will not be entitled to claim back* payments they made during the four weeks your property remained unsold.

After the 12 weeks, any help you receive from the local authority will be charged against the value of your property. You must pay this money back when you sell.

The value of your home doesn't count if these people need to go on living there

■ your husband, wife or unmarried partner

■ a close relative over 60 or under 16

■ a carer or a relative under 60 who is incapacitated

---

* If you are having problems obtaining funding from your local authority, you'll find more details in Help the Aged's free information sheet No. 27 *Paying for residential care: problems with local authority funding* or call their freephone advice line on **0808 800 6565**.

What happens if you have less than £20,000?

If you have capital below £20,000, or your savings after a few months of paying for care, are reduced to this level, you may be entitled to some help from the State towards your care costs.

You will be asked to claim any benefits to which you are entitled such as Income Support. These will be taken into account when working out how much you can afford to pay. Usually, you will have to pay all your income towards the fees less £18.10 a week which you keep for personal expenses.

If you have capital between £12,250 and £20,000 you pay £1 per week from your savings for each £250 of capital between those figures.

If you have capital below £12,250, you can claim the maximum state help.

Selling your home to pay for care

The value of your home counts towards your £20,000 limit. So you will usually be expected to sell it to pay the fees. If you cannot or do not wish to sell, the local authority may assist with your fees. But they will put a legal charge on your property and claim back what you owe when it is eventually sold.

You do not have to sell your home if certain people need to live there, see page 75.

Giving your home away to avoid paying fees

Deprivation of assets is when a person gives away what he owns in order to avoid fees for residential care. For example, a father gives his house to his son.

Be aware that

- a local authority can look back into your affairs. It may ask you (or the person to whom you gave your house) to pay if it thinks you have been trying to avoid payment
- you may never need residential care! Most people don't
- your home may be at risk if the person you gave it to mortgages it, divorces or goes bankrupt

Renting out your home to pay for care

The main advantages of renting out your home to pay for care are

- you have somewhere to come back to if the care home doesn't work out
- it may increase in value and can later be sold. You could then leave a legacy to friends, relatives or a good cause

The main disadvantage is that someone - agent, relative or friend - will have to handle the rental. And you need to set aside money to cover

- home fees during a rent-free period
- repairs, maintenance, decoration and insurance
- tax payable on rental income

What if you don't own your home but are a tenant?

If you enter a nursing and residential home for an indefinite period, you still have to pay rent on your house or flat while away.

A stay of up to 52 weeks in a care home is considered temporary. **It is up to your local authority whether or not to charge you for a stay of less than eight weeks**. After eight weeks, they should apply the means test rules described above. But they should allow you to keep as much income as you need to pay rent, council tax, service charge and other essentials.

If you are entering residential care permanently, you will be expected to give up your rented home when you move out.

Help with the cost of your nursing care

Even if you are a 'self-funder' so pay your nursing home fees out of your own funds, you are still entitled to some help towards the cost of your nursing care. Your local health authority will pay a portion of the costs.

How it works

Your local health authority decides how much nursing you need. They assess you either: before you are discharged from hospital, or at your nursing home. Depending on how much care you need, you qualify for a certain amount, currently £40, £77.50 or £125, off your weekly bill.

(The amounts and regulations are different if you live in Scotland, Wales or Northern Ireland - for details, phone one of the organisations listed on page 82.)

The nursing home claims this amount back from the health authority and should either refund you directly or deduct money from your bill.

No system works perfectly. If you think you are not getting the money off that you should, ask a friend or relative to contact your local health authority. They should ask for the nursing home fees contribution department, say who you are and where you live and request an assessment.

Read Help the Aged's information sheet No. 10 *Paying for Residential Care*. Tel: 020 7278 1114.

Residential & nursing home care

Charitable help towards care fees

There may be a charity such as IndependentAge which can help you pay for a residential or nursing home. See section 1, pages 13 and 14.

Insurance to pay care home fees

This kind of insurance is called long term care insurance. It pays a monthly benefit which you use either

■ to pay for professional nursing care in your own home
■ to pay home fees

You receive money as soon as the insured person fails a set number of 'activities of daily living' e.g. is no longer able to bath without help.

Factors to consider

■ you need to seek advice. But independent financial advisors may not be entirely impartial if they have a product to sell

■ you may never need residential care. Most people don't!

■ if you need financial help now, consider an immediate needs policy. Your relative can take out such a policy for you if they have Enduring Power of Attorney. Be sure to get quotations from several companies as prices can vary considerably

■ plans which pay benefits in full and in cash are the most flexible

Where to find out more

The **Nursing Home Fees Agency (NHFA)**
Long Term Care Guide. Freephone **0800 99 88 33** for a free copy.

The Observer's guide, **Finding and Funding a Care Home.**
Telephone: **0800 694 7007** for a free copy.

What to look for in a home

It's not unreasonable to expect a care home to be spotlessly clean, with genuinely caring staff and a friendly, homely atmosphere. And are the other residents the kind you could get along with? For a helpful checklist of what to look for in a home, call the Relatives' and Residents' Association on **020 7359 8136**.

> **It is easy to let emotions get in the way**
> Compile a list of questions to ask over the phone.
> This will help you to eliminate homes which do not meet your needs and could save you a visit.

Help and advice

Counsel and Care	can provide advice on finding and paying for residential care **www.counselandcare.org.uk**	local rate **0845 30 07 585**
Help the Aged Care Fees Advisory Service	gives free and impartial advice on paying for residential care **www.helptheaged.org.uk/carefees**	**0500 76 74 76**
The Cinnamon Trust	can provide a list of care homes willing to accept pets, or it may be able to look after a pet you can't take with you **www.cinnamon.org.uk**	**01736 757 900**
The Elderly Accommodation Counsel	keeps lists of private and voluntary accommodation for older people, by area and price range **www.housingcare.org**	**020 7820 1343**
The Nursing Home Fees Agency (NHFA)	provides free advice on how best to pay for care, publishes information sheets **www.nhfa.co.uk**	freephone **0800 99 88 33**
The Relatives' and Residents' Association	can provide advice on finding and paying for residential care as well as a checklist of things to look for **www.relres.org**	**020 7359 8136**

An independent life thanks to IndependentAge

IndependentAge is a national charity which helps older people on low incomes to stay in their own homes, whether owned or rented.

We can provide:

- a small income for life
- financial help in times of crisis
- equipment such as power bath seats, wheelchairs and stair lifts
- nursing and residential care and help with fees
- clothing and household linen
- the friendship and support of our volunteer visitors

"IndependentAge has given me back my security. I used to lie awake at night worrying about my bills until IndependentAge stepped in."

Mrs H, 78, Suffolk

"I look forward to visits from Mary. She gives me friendly advice and her conversation cheers me up."

Miss T, 75, Devon

"IndependentAge helped me to get my walker-trolley – I would be lost without it."

Mrs S, 83, Ayrshire

We cannot help everyone in need so we give priority to those who have helped others.

Find out more about IndependentAge by

- visiting our website **www.independentage.org.uk**
- or telephoning us on 020 7605 4200
- or by writing to Jonathan Powell, Chief Executive, IndependentAge, 6 Avonmore Road, London W14 8RL.

Can we help someone you know?

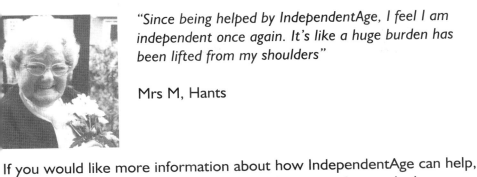

"Since being helped by IndependentAge, I feel I am independent once again. It's like a huge burden has been lifted from my shoulders"

Mrs M, Hants

If you would like more information about how IndependentAge can help, or are interested in joining our team of volunteers, please telephone our Care Officer on 020 7605 4200 or complete the form below. All enquiries are handled with discretion and in the strictest confidence.

I am interested in: (PLEASE TICK)

☐ **how IndependentAge can help someone I know**

☐ **how IndependentAge can help me**

☐ **becoming a volunteer**

Title (Mr/Mrs/Miss/Other)   First name (s)

Last name

Address

Postcode

Telephone

Please return the form to:

The Care Officer, IndependentAge, 6 Avonmore Road London W14 8RL

If you have found this guide useful, you may also be interested in *60-Wise at Home*.

Sir Roger Bannister CBE said,

'Even the fittest people sometimes find that things can become more difficult as they get older. This booklet from the charity IndependentAge provides lots of hints and tips that can help make life easier. We all want to remain independent for as long as possible. 60-Wise at Home is a useful and practical guide. It is written in a straightforward and easy-to-read style. So why not take its advice and stay independent for longer.'

'*60-Wise at Home*' gives information on help available:
- Around the house
- Relaxing in your living room
- Cooking and eating
- Comfort in your bedroom
- Independence in the bathroom
- Making the most of your garden
- Obtaining advice and products

For a copy of *60-Wise at Home*, please complete the form below.

Name

Address

Please return the form to: **60-Wise at Home, IndependentAge, 6 Avonmore Road, London W14 8RL**

The booklet is free but we would appreciate a donation towards our work helping older people in need to remain independent.

Please help

The charity **IndependentAge** helps people in financial difficulties who are over 65 years old, or over 40 and unable to resume work due to physical disability. Our main aim is to enable older people to retain their independence. Please support our work.

☐   I would like to make a donation of £ _____

☐   I enclose my cheque (payable to **IndependentAge**) or

☐   Please charge my credit card (Visa/Mastercard)

Card number: ☐☐☐☐ ☐☐☐☐ ☐☐☐☐ ☐☐☐☐

Expiry date: ☐☐ ☐☐

☐   **Gift Aid**. Please tick here if you would like **IndependentAge** to reclaim the tax you have paid on this and any future donations (making them worth 28% more at no extra cost to you). You must have paid income or capital gains tax at least equal to the amount being reclaimed. You are under no obligation to make any further donations and you may cancel this declaration at any time.

Signature _____ Date _____

Mr/Mrs/Ms/Other _____

Name _____

Address _____

_____

Postcode _____

Supporting older people at home

Please use an envelope and send to
IndependentAge, 6 Avonmore Road, London W14 8RL.